VOID

Words •
Kalagata

Images •
Superimposition

2025

Words by Kalagata
Images by Superimposition
www.visualsoma.com

First Published 2025
Mindless Books • Springvale

MIND
LESS

contents		
	01	clouds
	02	concrete
	03	subject
	04	jungle
	05	mirror
	06	world
	07	traffic
	08	crack
	09	shadows
	10	void
	11	egos
	12	screen
	13	substratum
	14	mortality
	15	river
	16	onion
	17	bunker
	18	room
	19	snake
	20	ink
	21	videotape
	22	ocean

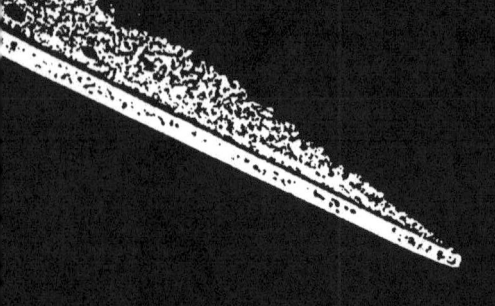

VOID :

1

the primordial state before creation.
an infinite field of pure potentiality,
from which all existence appears.

2

nothingness, emptiness, or a complete
absence of being.

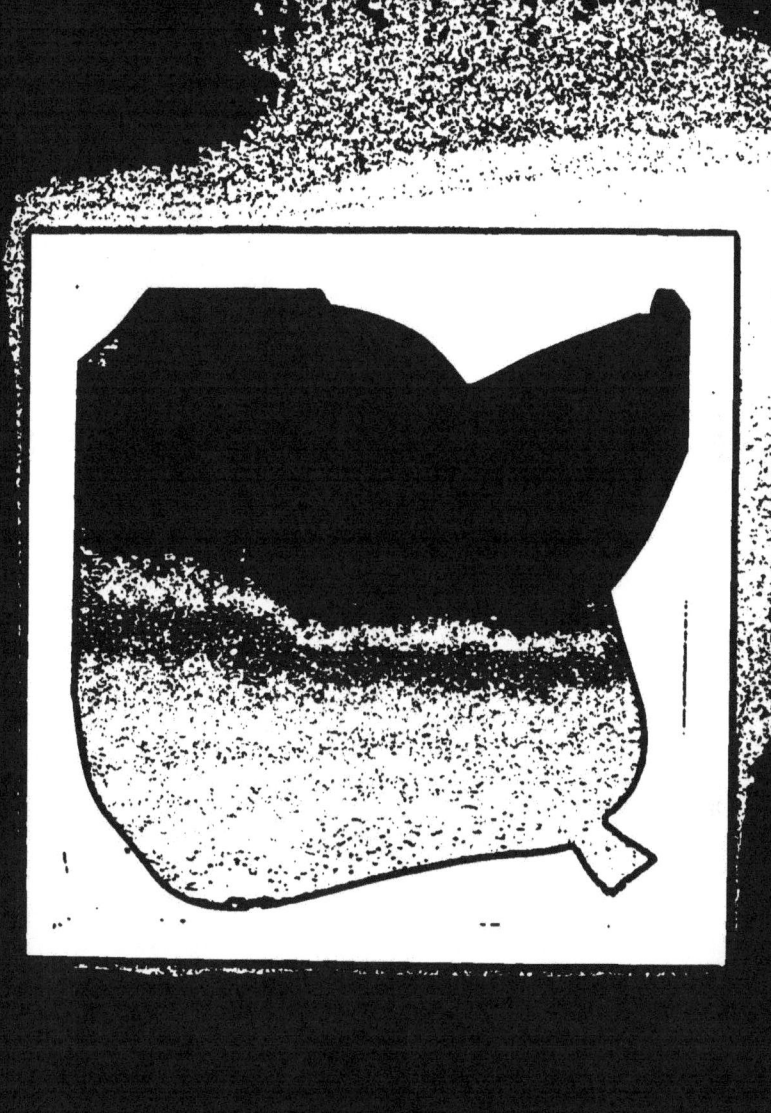

01

the primitive buzz
retrospective clouds passing
pesky temptation

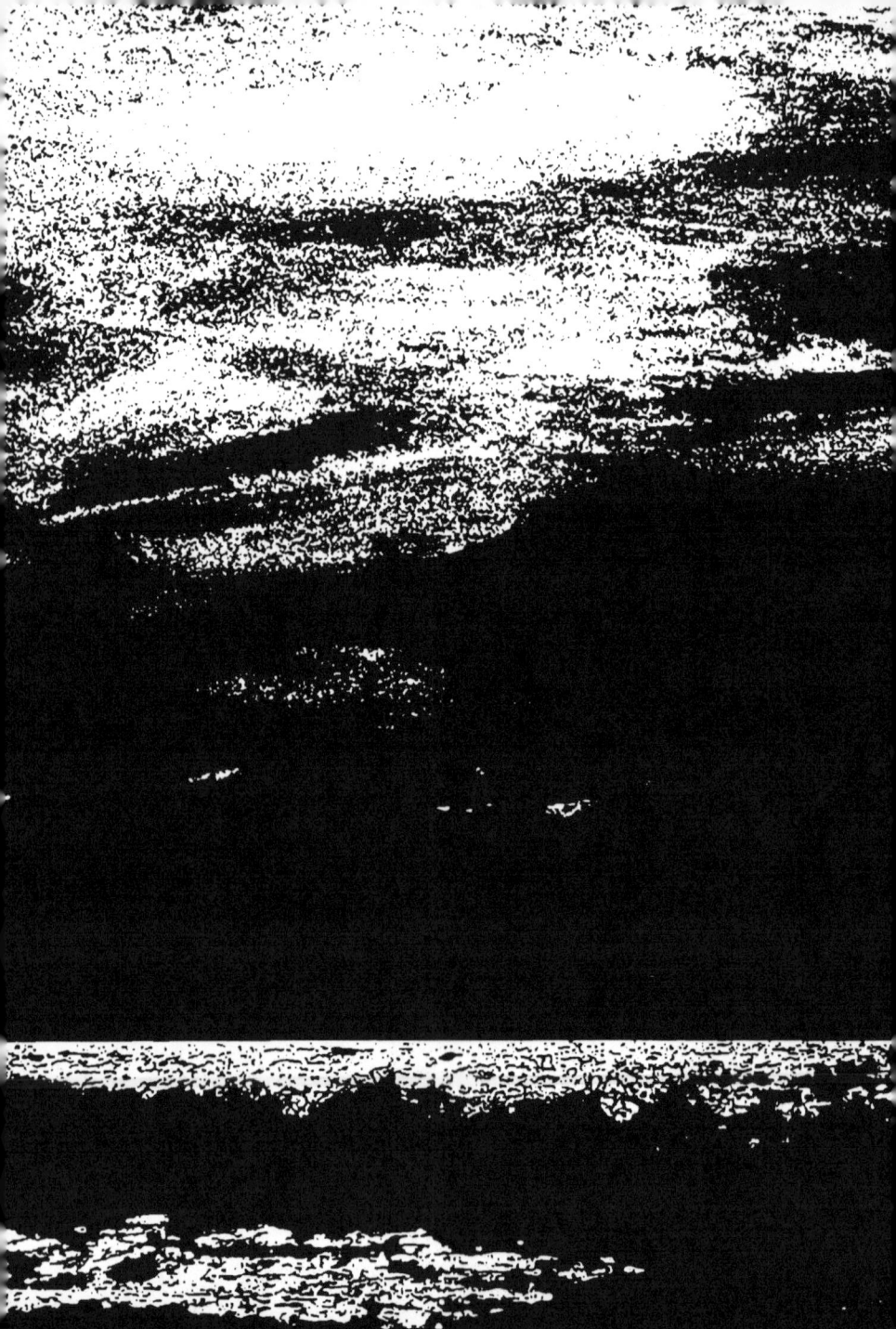

02

fleeting dream deceit
name and form unrelenting
the idea concrete

03

subject objected
untouchable divided
seer becomes seen

04

night jungle fruitless
continuous circle lines
branding the fire

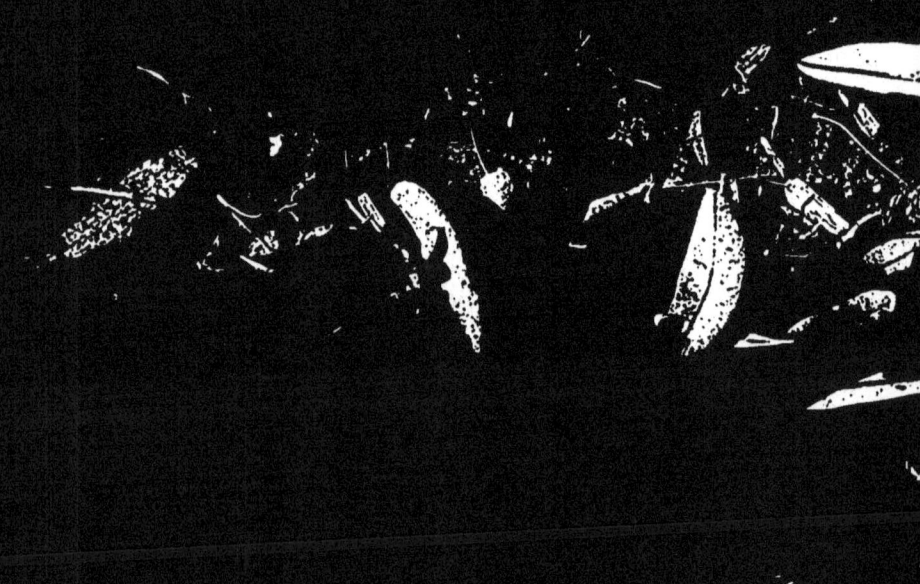

abandoned perspectives

05

fixed mirror broken
rear city view and the six
jugglers of sensation

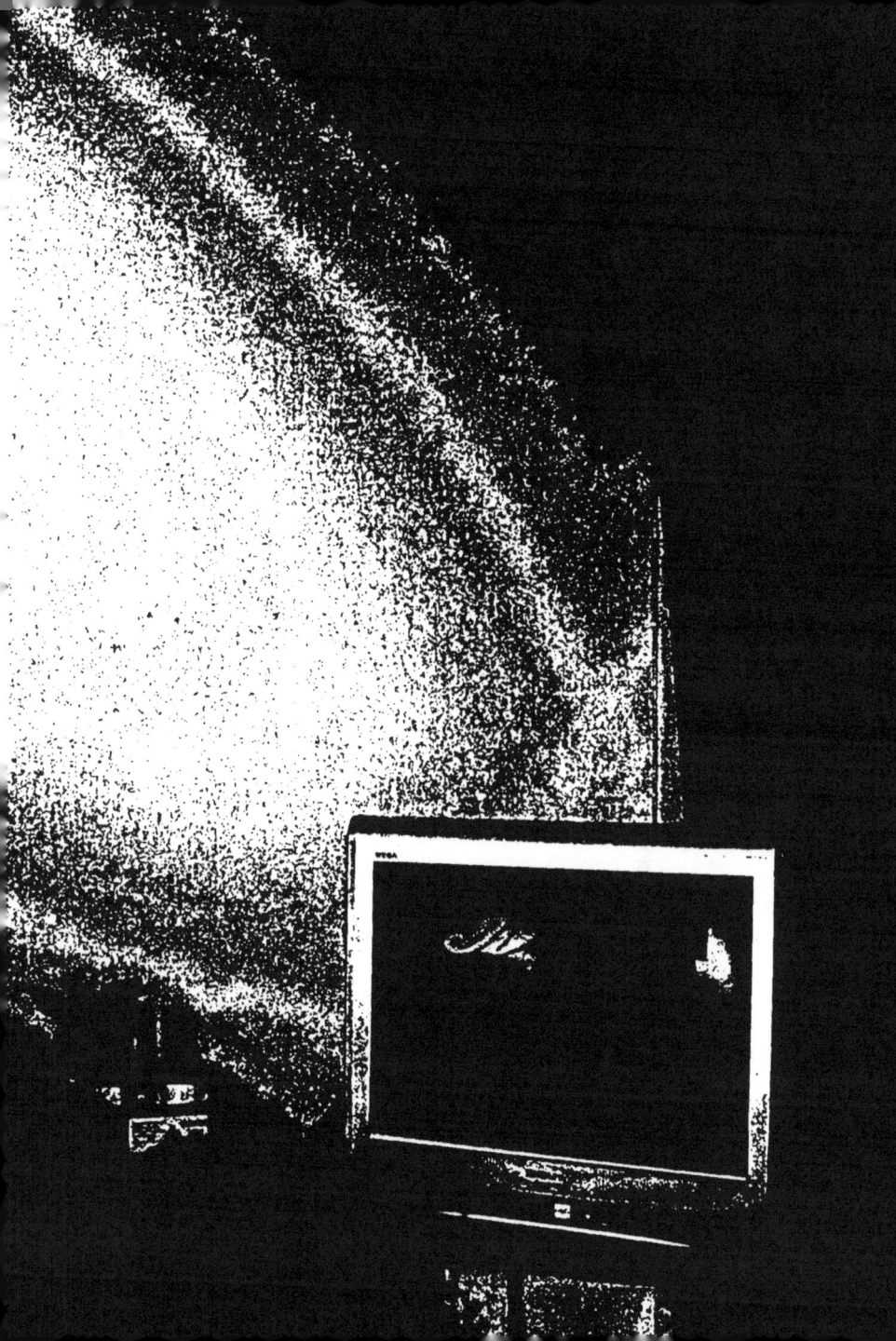

in the
beginningless

06

the thought world appears
a reactionary fear
the origin myth

07

sunlit figment leaves
traffic weaves the infinite
snare of attraction

knower and the unknown

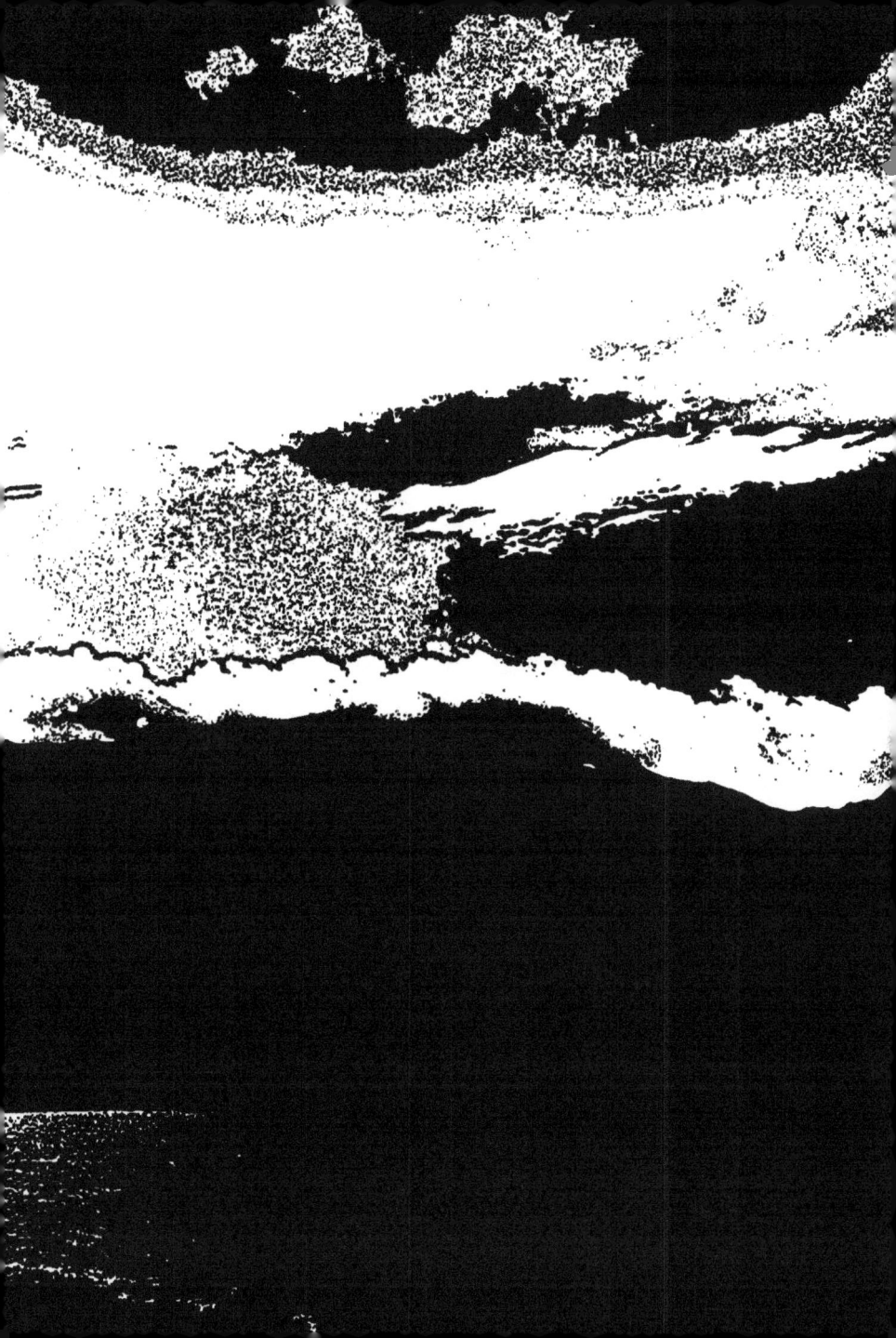

09

ecliptic shadows
the moment misrepresents
a lent existence test

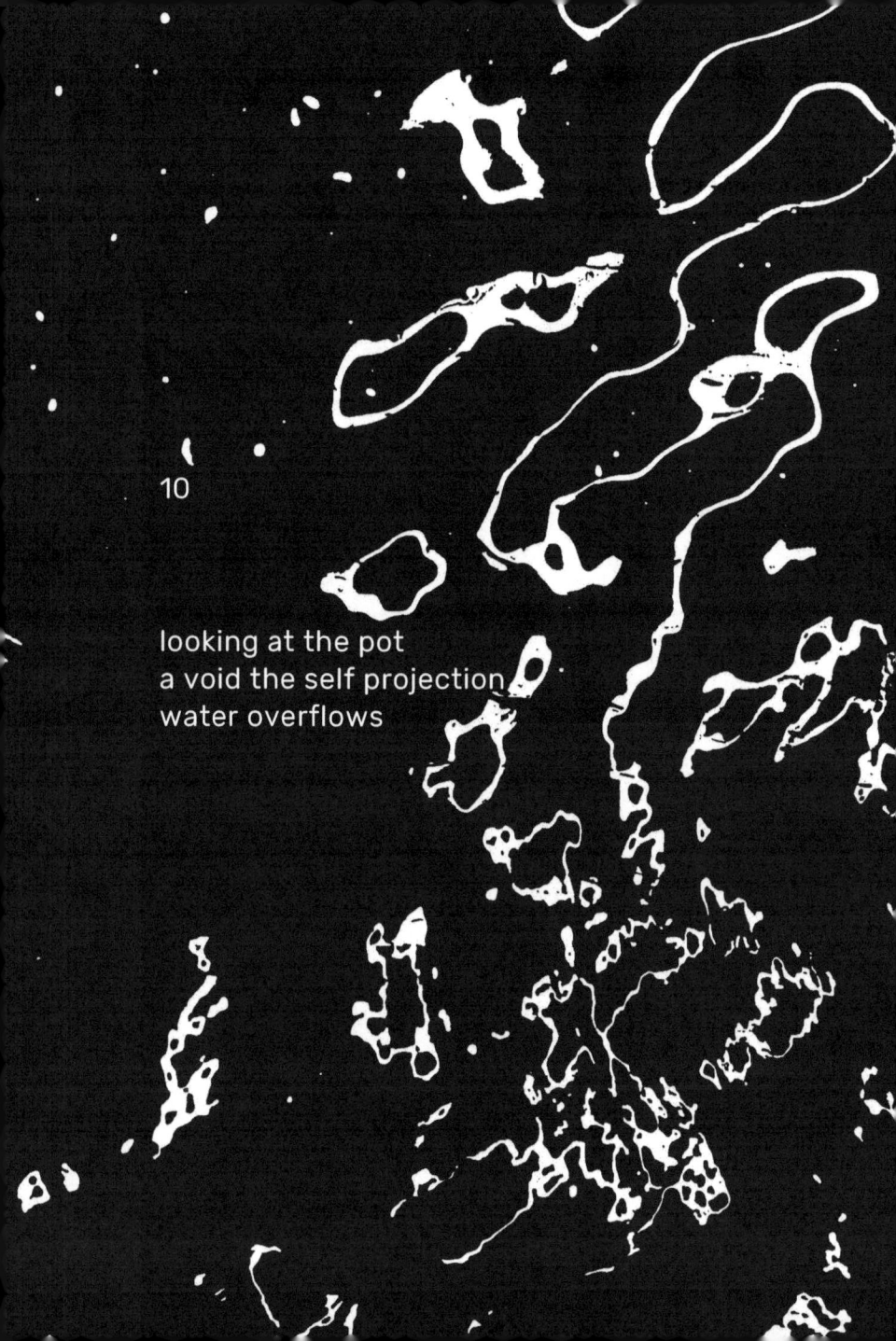

10

looking at the pot
a void the self projection
water overflows

11

juggernaut behold
who is playing a role to
satisfy egos

opening curtains
reveal screen reflection
amusing reruns

12

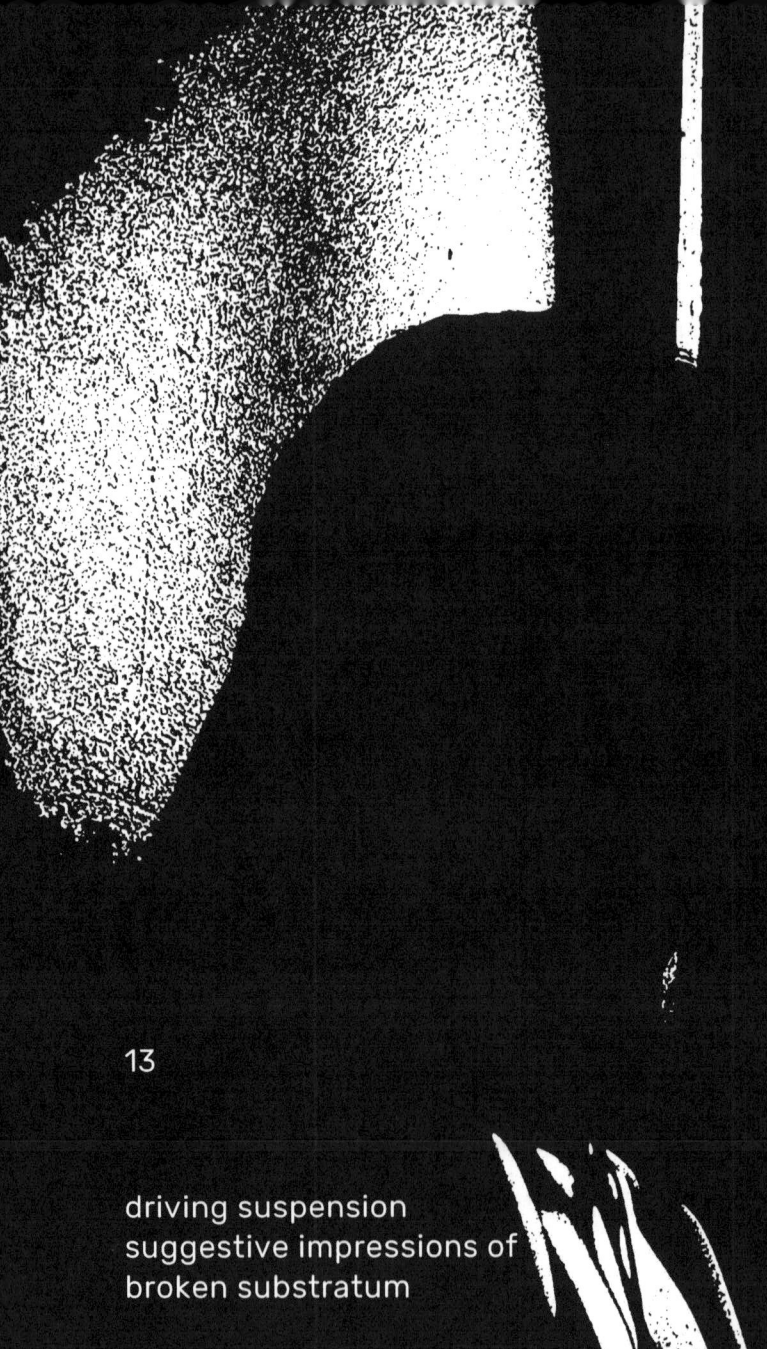

13

driving suspension
suggestive impressions of
broken substratum

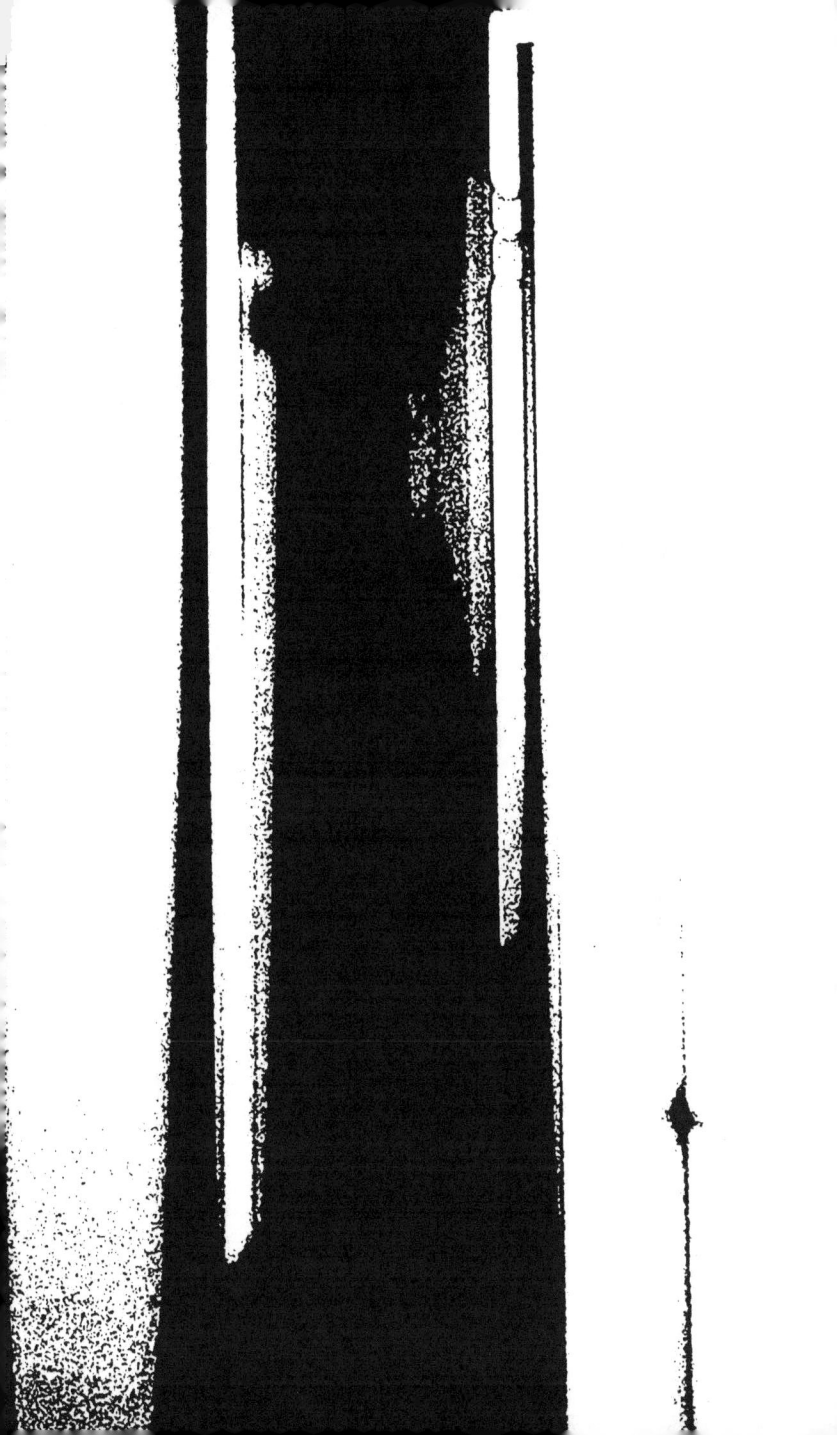

arriving empty
naive or fake why wait
try mortality

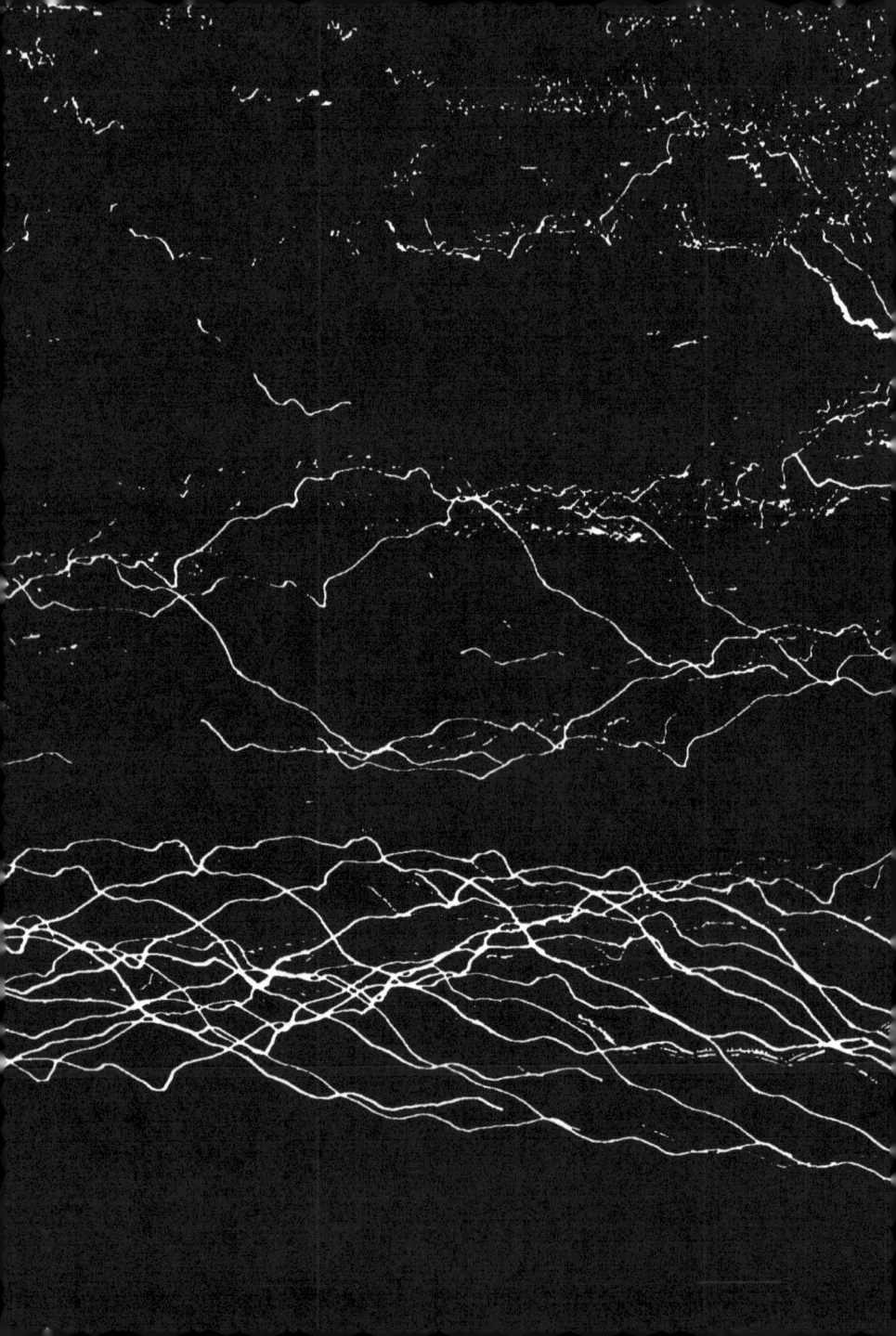

crossing the river
counting for old mate the tenth
loss self evident

16

opinionated
unnecessary onion
the thought of burden

17

a busy body
existence consciousness bliss
sat in a bunker

18

waiting room vacant
that sentimentality
transition to fool

19

rope mistaken snake
phantoms feed the mind till late
absolute charade

going
nowhere

20

new page
more ink
still nothing

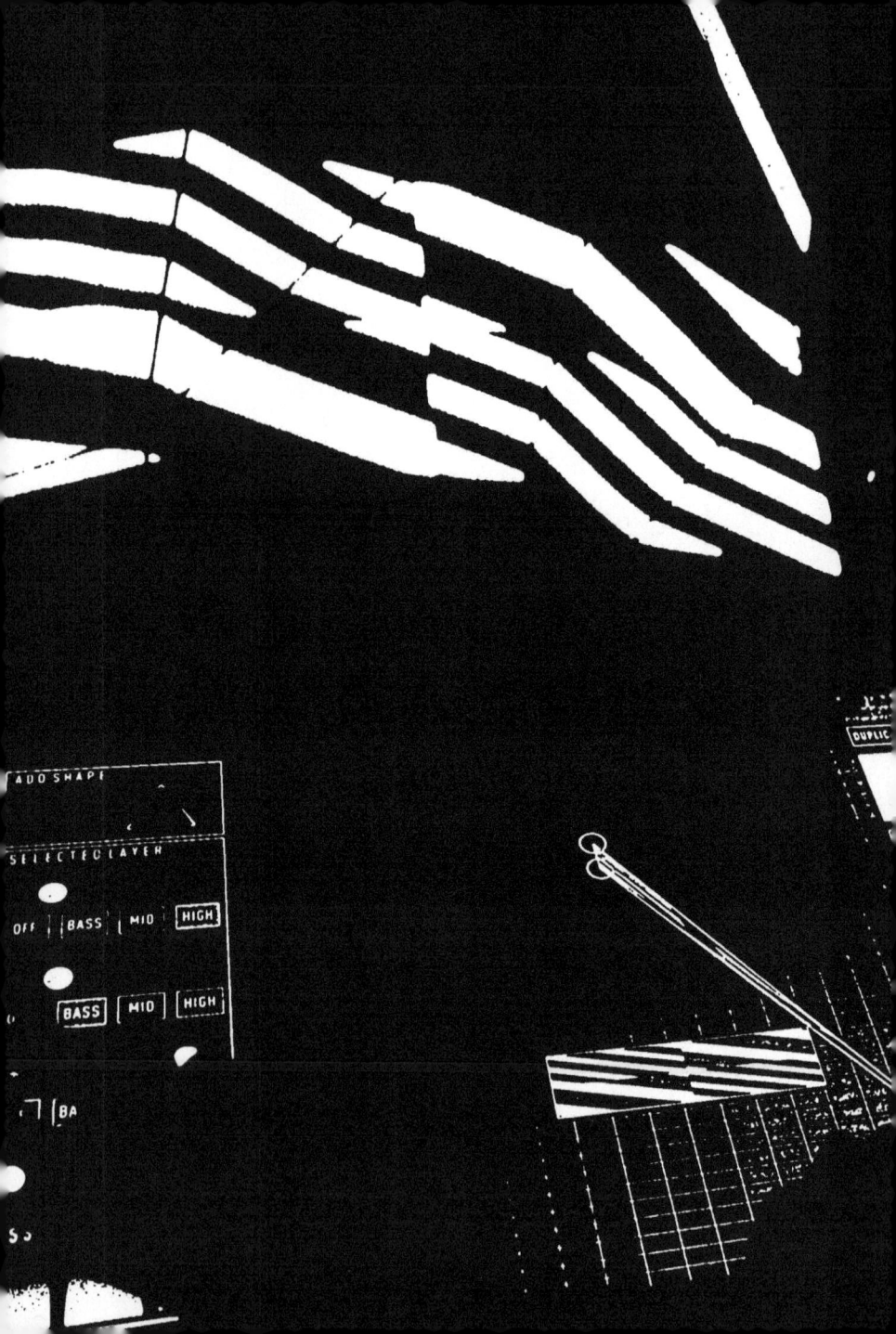

21

no faith unknown time
invested in disbeliefs
rewind videotape

full moon haze potion
thick night gazing over soon
empty the ocean

www.ingramcontent.com/pod-product-compliance
Lightning Source LLC
Chambersburg PA
CBHW061212070526
44583CB00025B/3215